Cool Hotels
Europe

teNeues

Editor:	Martin Nicholas Kunz
Editorial coordination:	Ulrike Paul
Introduction:	Christian Schönwetter
Translations:	Ade Team, Robert Kaplan (English), Ludovic Allain (French), Margarita Celdràn-Kuhl (Spanish)
Art-director:	Thomas Hausberg
Layout:	Cornelia Stockhausen
Imaging:	Jan Hausberg
Maps & Pre-press:	go4media. – Verlagsbüro, Stuttgart

Published by teNeues Publishing Group

teNeues Publishing Company
16 West 22nd Street, New York, NY 10010, USA
Tel.: 001-212-627-9090, Fax: 001-212-627-9511

teNeues Book Division
Kaistraße 18
40221 Düsseldorf, Germany
Tel.: 0049-(0)211-994597-0, Fax: 0049-(0)211-994597-40

teNeues Publishing UK Ltd.
P.O. Box 402
West Byfleet
KT14 7ZF, Great Britain
Tel.: 0044-1932-403509, Fax: 0044-1932-403514

teNeues France S.A.R.L.
4, rue de Valence
75005 Paris, France
Phone: 0033-1-55 76 62 05, Fax: 0033-1-55 76 64 19

www.teneues.com

ISBN: 3-8238-4582-9

© 2004 teNeues Verlag GmbH + Co. KG, Kempen

Printed in Italy

Bibliographic information published by Die Deutsche
Bibliothek. Die Deutsche Bibliothek lists this publication
in the Deutsche Nationalbibliografie; detailed bibliographic
data is available in the Internet at http://dnb.ddb.de

Content

Introduction   8

Iceland
                    Reykjavik   101 hotel   20
Estonia
                    Tallinn   The Three Sisters Hotel   26
Sweden
                    Gothenburg   Elite Plaza Hotel   36
                    Stockholm   Hotel J Nacka Strand   40
Denmark
                    Copenhagen   Skt. Petri   46
Ireland
                    Dublin   The Morrison   52
United Kingdom
                    London   No. 5 Maddox Street   58
                                 The Metropolitan   64
                                 Guesthouse West   72
                                 Myhotel Chelsea   78
                    Manchester   Alias Rossetti   82
The Netherlands
                    Maastricht   La Bergère   88

Germany

Berlin	Ku'damm 101 Hotel	98
	Q!	104
	Radisson SAS	112
Frankfurt	Steigenberger Metropolitan	118
	Bristol Hotel	122
Hamburg	25h	128
Helgoland	atoll	136
Munich	Palace	144

Switzerland

Geneva	Hôtel La Réserve	148
Luzern	The Hotel	150
Zurich	Greulich	158
	Widder	164

Austria

Ischgl	Madlein	170
Vienna	Hanner	180

France

Nice	Hi Hôtel	190
Corsica	Hotel Casadelmar	196
Paris	Bel Ami	206
	Park Hyatt Vendome	212
	Pershing Hall	218

Italy

Florence	Continentale	226
	Gallery Hotel Art	234
Milan	Town House 31	240
	The Gray	246
	St Raf	256
	Park Hyatt Milan	262
Padua	Methis Hotel	268
Rome	Hotel Art	274
	es.hotel	282
Sardinia	Hotel La Coluccia	290
South Tirol	Vigilius Mountain Resort	298
Venice	Charming House DD.724	308

Spain

	Barcelona	Hotel Neri	316
		Prestige Hotel Paseo de Gracia	324
		Capital	334
		Hotel Omm	342
	Bilbao	Miró Hotel	350
	Madrid	AC Santo Mauro	356
	Majorca	Convent de la Missio	364
		Maricel	370
		Son Brull Hotel & Spa	380

Greece

| | Athens | Semiramis Hotel | 386 |

Turkey

| | Istanbul | Bentley | 392 |

| Architects/Designers | | | 398 |
| Photo Credits | | | 399 |

Introduction

Where are we heading? Not only businesspersons and vacationers pose this question; hoteliers pose themselves this question too: where are we headed when furnishing and designing a hotel? Which tendencies exist when conceiving new accommodations? What must one think about nowadays so the guests will also come tomorrow?

An important trend, evolving for some time, is the development away from conformity and towards individuality. Just as a particular style no longer reigns in the world of fashion but many styles exist next to each other and individuals choose what fits them best based on their personal preferences in order to underscore their own personality, hotels are also increasingly fashioned very individually in order to impart the guest a unique experience.

Architects and designers create locations with widely differing characters. Some interiors stand out from the masses through highly topical, modernistic, perhaps rather stylish design, while others surpass rather through their timeless strictness and asceticism. The planners then often try to let the spirit of the locality, the character of the city in which the accommodation is found, be felt even in the rooms. They challenge the interchangeable run-of-the-mill furnishings of the hotel chains that let every traveler forget exactly where he is. Rather, they imagine a hotel room as the design ideal, even if it can never be accomplished in its pure form, in which the guest immediately recognizes the city in which he is residing when he lets his first drowsy glance roam around the room even upon awakening.

However, as not only the ambience but also the service contribute to individualization, some hotels offer specials that are tailored to target groups interested in art, architecture, and design. Thus, a Berlin hotel lures with a total package that includes not only overnight stays in avant-garde designed rooms but also admission to the Jewish Museum by the star architect Daniel Libeskind.

Demanding customers who are not content with mass-produced goods in all areas of life but rather place value on something special will know to appreciate this. They seek that which is exceptional not only at home but also on the way—regardless of where they are headed.

Christian Schönwetter

Einleitung

Wohin geht die Reise? Diese Frage stellen sich nicht nur Geschäftsleute und Urlauber, diese Frage stellen sich auch Hoteliers: Wohin geht die Reise bei der Einrichtung und Gestaltung von Hotels? Welche Tendenzen gibt es bei der Konzeption neuer Unterkünfte? Was muss man sich heute einfallen lassen, damit die Gäste auch morgen kommen?

Ein wichtiger Trend, der sich seit einiger Zeit abzeichnet, ist die Entwicklung weg von der Konformität hin zur Individualität. So wie in der Mode seit Jahren nicht mehr ein Stil vorherrscht, sondern viele Stile nebeneinander existieren, und der Einzelne sich nach persönlichen Vorlieben das für sich Passende heraussucht, um seine Persönlichkeit zu unterstreichen, so werden auch Hotels verstärkt ganz individuell gestaltet, um dem Gast ein einzigartiges Erlebnis zu vermitteln.

Architekten und Designer schaffen Orte ganz unterschiedlichen Charakters. Manche Interieurs heben sich durch hochaktuelle, poppige, vielleicht gar modische Gestaltung von der Masse ab, während andere eher durch ihre zeitlose Strenge und Askese aus dem Rahmen fallen. Der Planer bemüht sich dabei häufig, den Geist des Ortes, den Charakter der Stadt, in der sich eine Unterkunft befindet, auch in deren Räumen spürbar zu machen. Er sagt der austauschbaren Allerweltsausstattung der Hotelketten, die jeden Vielreisenden vergessen lässt, wo er sich gerade befindet, den Kampf an. Als Gestaltungsideal, das natürlich nie in Reinform verwirklicht werden kann, schwebt ihm stattdessen ein Hotelzimmer vor, bei dem der Gast schon beim Aufwachen, wenn er seinen ersten schlaftrunkenen Blick durchs Zimmer schweifen lässt, sofort erkennt, in welcher Stadt er sich aufhält.

Weil jedoch nicht nur das Ambiente zur Individualisierung beiträgt, sondern auch der Service, bieten einige Hotels Specials an, die auf eine kunst-, architektur- und designinteressierte Zielgruppe zugeschnitten sind. So lockt ein Berliner Haus mit einem Gesamtpaket, das nicht nur Übernachtungen in avantgardistisch gestalteten Zimmern, sondern auch den Eintritt in das Jüdische Museum des Stararchitekten Daniel Libeskind mit einschließt.

Anspruchsvolle Kunden, die sich in allen Lebensbereichen nicht mit Massenware begnügen, sondern Wert auf etwas Besonderes legen, werden dies zu schätzen wissen. Sie suchen das Außergewöhnliche nicht nur zu Hause, sondern auch unterwegs – ganz egal, wohin die Reise geht.

Christian Schönwetter

Introduction

Où allons-nous ? Cette question, les hommes, les femmes d'affaires et les vacanciers ne sont pas les seuls à se la poser. Les professionnels de l'hôtellerie aussi : dans quelle direction en effet aménager et décorer les hôtels ? Quelles tendances présideront-elles à la conception des nouveaux hébergements ? Quelles idées faut-il transposer aujourd'hui pour que les hôtes reviennent demain ?

Une tendance importante se dessine depuis quelques temps, marquant la fin du conformisme pour laisser place à l'individualisme. A l'instar de la mode où l'on voit depuis des années prévaloir non plus un style, mais se côtoyer plusieurs styles à la fois, avec la liberté pour chacun de choisir celui qui lui convient, les hôtels seront plus souvent aménagés avec une note d'individualité très marquée, pour que le client reparte avec un bagage de souvenirs unique en son genre.

Les architectes et concepteurs créent des sites aux caractères très différents les uns des autres. Nombre d'intérieurs se détachent de la masse par leur décoration très actuelle, bigarrée, voire à la mode, tandis que d'autres sortent de l'ordinaire par une rigueur et un ascétisme décoratifs détachés du temps. Souvent l'architecte s'efforce de faire revivre aussi dans les pièces l'esprit du lieu, l'atmosphère de la ville dans laquelle se trouve l'hôtel. Il entre en lutte ouverte contre ce mobilier interchangeable rencontré dans les chaînes hôtelières et qui fait oublier aux voyageurs fréquents le nom de la ville où ils se trouvent ponctuellement. Pour l'architecte d'intérieur, l'aménagement idéal, irréalisable naturellement en sa forme pure, est celui qui permet au visiteur

encore ensommeillé de se rappeler, dès son premier regard matinal par la fenêtre, le nom de la ville dans laquelle il séjourne.

Vu que non seulement l'ambiente architectural mais aussi le service contribuent à l'individualisation, certains hôtels offrent des Specials conçus à l'intention d'un groupe-cible intéressé par l'art, l'architecture et le design. Ainsi une adresse berlinoise invite-t-elle à une prestation complète incluant non seulement des nuités dans des chambres aux décorations d'avant-garde, mais encore une entrée au Musée Juif dessiné par une star de l'architecture, Daniel Libeskind.

Les clients exigeants, ceux qui dans tous les domaines de l'existence ne sauraient se satisfaire du matérialisme de masse et qui vouent de l'importance à l'originalité, sauront apprécier. Ces clients recherchent des ambiances exceptionnelles non seulement chez eux mais encore en voyage, où qu'ils aillent.

Christian Schönwetter

Introducción

¿Cuál es la tendencia ahora? Esta pregunta no sólo se la hacen comerciantes y vacacionistas, la pregunta se la hacen también los hoteleros: ¿Cuál es la tendencia en instalaciones y diseño de hoteles? ¿Qué tendencias hay en la concepción de nuevos alojamientos? ¿Qué se tiene hoy que tener en cuenta para que los huéspedes sigan viniendo mañana?

Una importante tendencia que destaca desde hace algún tiempo es una evolución alejada de la conformidad y cada vez más individualizada. Así como en la moda hace ya años que no predomina un estilo, sino que coexisten muchos estilos y el individuo, para remarcar su personalidad, escoge aquello que se ajusta a su preferencia personal, así los hoteles se diseñan de forma notoriamente individualizada para proporcionar al huésped una experiencia única.

Arquitectos y diseñadores crean lugares de muy diverso carácter. Algunos interiores se diferencian de la masa por su estilo vanguardista, moderno, acaso muy a la moda, mientras que otros destacan más bien por su austeridad y ascetismo intemporal. Así, el planificador se preocupa a menudo por plasmar sensiblemente también en las estancias del alojamiento el espíritu del lugar y el carácter de la ciudad en la que aquel se encuentra. Declara la guerra al estilo omnipresente en todo el mundo e intercambiable de las cadenas hoteleras, que hace olvidar a cualquier viajero asiduo dónde se halla. En vez de éste, como ideal de diseño –que naturalmente nunca podrá realizarse en toda su pureza– tiene en mente una habitación de hotel en la que el huésped, nada más

despertarse, cuando deja vagar su primera mirada aún adormilada por la habitación, reconoce de inmediato en qué ciudad se encuentra.

Puesto que no sólo el ambiente contribuye a la individualización, sino que también lo hace el servicio, algunos hoteles ofrecen especiales dirigidos particularmente a grupos de destino interesados en el arte, la arquitectura y el diseño. Así, una casa berlinesa atrae con un paquete completo que no incluye sólo pernoctas en habitaciones de estilo vanguardista, sino también la entrada al Museo Judío del arquitecto estrella Daniel Libeskind.

Los clientes exigentes que no se conforman en ningún ámbito de la vida con un producto para la masa, sino que conceden importancia a lo especial aprenderán a valorar esto. Buscan lo extraordinario no sólo en casa, sino también cuando viajan, sin que importe cuál sea la tendencia.

Christian Schönwetter

Introduzione

Dove ci porta il viaggio? Non soltanto uomini d'affari e viaggiatori si pongono questa domanda, ma anche albergatori: Dove ci porta il viaggio nell'arredamento e la decorazione degli hotel? Quali sono le tendenze nella concezione di nuovi alloggi? Quali sono le idee che bisogna avere oggi per vedere arrivare gli ospiti anche domani?

Un trend importante che da poco si sta mettendo in evidenza consiste nell'allontanarsi dal conformismo per orientarsi verso l'individualismo. Così come nella moda da anni non prevale soltanto uno stile, ma coesistono molti stili ed ogni individuo può scegliere quello che secondo i suoi gusti gli sta meglio per sottolineare la propria personalità, così anche gli hotel vengono creati in modo sempre più individuale per regalare all'ospite un'esperienza unica.

Architetti e designer creano posti del tutto diversi tra loro. Alcuni arredamenti interni si distinguono dalla massa grazie all'essere di grande attualità, sgargianti o forse addirittura alla moda, mentre altri escono dagli schemi per la loro eterna austerità e ascesi. Il disegnatore spesso cerca di rendere tangibile nelle camere lo spirito del posto, il carattere della città dove si trova l'alloggio. Dichiara guerra all'arredamento dal gusto comune ed intercambiabile delle grandi catene di alberghi che fanno dimenticare al viaggiatore frequente dove si trova. Porta in mente un ideale della creazione – che naturalmente non si lascia mai realizzare nella sua forma più pura – di una camera d'albergo dove l'ospite aprendo gli occhi al risveglio e lasciando scorrere lo sguardo riesce a riconoscere immediatamente in quale città si trova.

Visto che non soltanto l'ambiente contribuisce a distinguersi, ma anche il servizio, alcuni hotel offrono servizi che sono tagliati su misura di una clientela interessata all'arte, l'architettura ed il design. Ad esempio ona casa di Berlino attira la clientela con un pacchetto globale che non comprende soltanto il pernottamento in una camera creata all'avanguardia, ma anche l'entrata al museo ebreo creato dall'architetto star Daniel Libeskind.

Clienti esigenti i quali in nessun settore della vita si accontentano della merce di gran consumo, dando invece importanza a qualcosa di particolare, lo sapranno apprezzare. Loro cercano lo straordinario non soltanto a casa, ma anche in viaggio – indipendentemente dove li porta.

Christian Schönwetter

Northern Europe

Iceland
Estonia
Sweden
Denmark
Ireland
United Kingdom
The Netherlands

Reykjavik
101 hotel

Copenhagen
Skt. Petri

Stockholm
Hotel J Nacka Strand

Tallinn
The Three Sisters Hotel

Gothenburg
Elite Plaza Hotel

Maastricht
La Bergère

London
No. 5 Maddox Street
The Metropolitan
Guesthouse West
Myhotel Chelsea

Manchester
Alias Rossetti

Dublin
The Morrison

101 hotel

Address:	Hverfisgata 10
	101 Reykjavík
Phone:	+354 580 01 01
Fax:	+354 580 01 00
Website:	www.101hotel.is
e-mail:	101hotel@101hotel.is
Located:	in downtown Reykjavik near government and cultural buildings, shops and nightlife, next door to the Iceland Opera House
Style:	stylish, elegant
Special features:	boardroom for 10-12 people
	fitness center, Jeep safaris, snowmobiles
Rooms:	38 rooms and suites
Opening date:	2002
Architecture / Design:	Ingibjörg Pálmadóttir

The Three Sisters Hotel

Address:	Pikk 71/Tolli 2
	10133 Tallinn
Phone:	+372 63 063 00
Fax:	+372 63 063 01
Website:	www.threesistershotel.com
e-mail:	info@threesistershotel.com
Located:	in the old town of Tallinn just a few steps from the Town Hall Square
Style:	contemporary
Special features:	restaurant Bordoo, bar Cloud Seven, wine cellar, The Tea Room, courtyard garden
	2 conferencing rooms for up to 70 people
Rooms:	23 rooms including 4 suites
Opening date:	2003
Architecture / Design:	Martinus Schuurman
	Külli Salum

The Morrison

Address:	Ormond Quay Dublin 1
Phone:	+353 1 887 24 00
Fax:	+353 1 878 31 85
Website:	www.morrisonhotel.ie
e-mail:	info@morrisonhotel.ie
Located:	in the heart of the city, walking distance of Temple Bar and Financial District
Style:	sleek, comfortable, contemporary
Special features:	2 restaurants, Morrison Bar and Café Bar Lobo conferencing room for up to 350 people garden room, also for private cocktail parties or meetings
Rooms:	84 superior rooms, 6 suites and a penthouse
Opening date:	1999
Architecture / Design:	Douglas I Wallace Architects and Designers

No. 5 Maddox Street

Address:	5 Maddox Street, Mayfair London W1S 2QD
Phone:	+44 20 76 47 02 00
Fax:	+44 20 76 47 03 00
Website:	www.no5maddoxst.com
e-mail:	no5maddoxst@living-rooms.co.uk
Located:	5 minutes from Soho or Mayfair, in the heart of Central London
Style:	contemporary, comfortable
Special features:	link with private gym, complimentary welcome tray, Molton Brown's new Somo skincare range
Rooms:	12 suites with private kitchen area
Opening date:	1999
Architecture / Design:	Baker Neville Design

The Metropolitan

Address:	19 Old Park Lane, Mayfair London W1K 1LB
Phone:	+44 20 74 47 10 00
Fax:	+44 20 74 47 11 00
Website:	www.metropolitan.co.uk
e-mail:	res@designhotels.com
Located:	in the center of London overlooking Hyde Park
Style:	timeless, contemporary
Special features:	restaurant and sushi bar Nobu, Met bar meeting rooms for up to 60 people
Rooms:	155 rooms including 18 suites
Opening date:	1997
Architecture / Design:	United Designers Keith Hobbs Linzi Coppick

Guesthouse West

Address:	163-165 Westbourne Grove, Notting Hill London W11 2RS
Phone:	+44 20 77 92 98 00
Fax:	+44 20 77 92 97 97
Website:	www.guesthousewest.com
e-mail:	enquiries@guesthousewest.com
Located:	in the heart of the exclusive Notting Hill area of London, 1 km from Paddington Station, 20 km from Heathrow Airport
Style:	natural, intimate
Special features:	bar, terrace
Rooms:	20 rooms
Opening date:	2004
Architecture / Design:	Francesca Mills

Address:	35 Ixworth Place, Chelsea
	London SW3 3QZ
Phone:	+44 20 72 25 75 00
Website:	www.myhotels.co.uk
e-mail:	mychelsea@myhotels.co.uk
Located:	in the stylish Brompton Cross shopping district,
	surrounded by designer boutiques, gift shops and
	restaurants
Style:	unique, individual
Special features:	mybar, 2 private dining rooms
Rooms:	45 rooms, studios and suites
Opening date:	2004
Architecture / Design:	James Soane from Project Orange

Alias Rossetti

Address:	107 Piccadilly Manchester M1 2DB
Phone:	+44 161 247 77 44
Fax:	+44 161 247 77 47
Website:	www.aliasrossetti.com
e-mail:	info@aliasrossetti.com
Located:	in the heart of Manchester only a minute away from Picadilly train station
Style:	hip, ultra-cool
Special features:	Café Paradiso 3 meeting rooms for 10 up to 200 people
Rooms:	61 rooms and 5 penthouses
Opening date:	2003
Architecture / Design:	Childs and Sulzman Nigel Chapman Interior design team – in house

La Bergère

Address:	Stationsstraat 40
	6221 Maastricht
Phone:	+31 4 33 28 25 25
Fax:	+31 4 33 28 25 26
Website:	www.la-bergere.com
e-mail:	info@la-bergere.com
Located:	in the city center, close to the entertainment and shopping area, 100 m from the train station, 10 km from Maastricht Aachen Airport, 15 minutes walk from Maastricht Conference Center
Style:	individual, tranquil
Special features:	espresso bar, wine bar, authentic Spanish tapas buffet, roof-top gym, La Byb library and reading room, beauty lounge
Rooms:	60 design rooms, 15 deluxe rooms, 50 apartments
Opening date:	reopened 2001
Architecture / Design:	Feran Thomassen

Central Europe

Germany
Switzerland
Austria
France

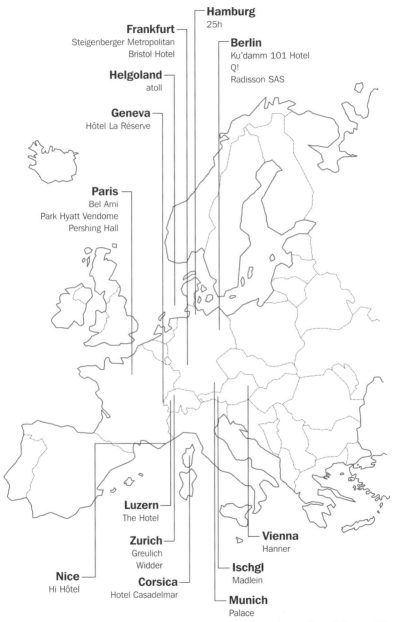

Hamburg
25h

Frankfurt
Steigenberger Metropolitan
Bristol Hotel

Berlin
Ku'damm 101 Hotel
Q!
Radisson SAS

Helgoland
atoll

Geneva
Hôtel La Réserve

Paris
Bel Ami
Park Hyatt Vendome
Pershing Hall

Luzern
The Hotel

Vienna
Hanner

Zurich
Greulich
Widder

Ischgl
Madlein

Nice
Hi Hôtel

Corsica
Hotel Casadelmar

Munich
Palace

Central Europe **97**

Ku'damm 101 Hotel

Address:	Kurfürstendamm 101
	10711 Berlin
Phone:	+49 30 520 05 50
Fax:	+49 30 520 05 55 55
Website:	www.kudamm101.de
e-mail:	info@kudamm101.com
Located:	near to Kurfürstendamm, ICC and exhibition center
Style:	stylish, caring, central
Special features:	breakfast restaurant, Loung Bar, catering service
	5 meeting rooms for up to 120 people,
	3 conferences suites for up to 12 people
Rooms:	171 rooms
Opening date:	2003
Architecture / Design:	Eyl, Weitz, Würmle & Partner
	Kadel-Quick-Scheib
	Kessler + Kessler

Q!

Address:	Knesebeckstraße 67
	10623 Berlin
Phone:	+49 30 810 06 60
Fax:	+49 30 810 06 66 66
Website:	www.loock-hotels.com
e-mail:	q-berlin@loock-hotels.com
Located:	directly at Kurfürstendamm
Style:	inspiring
Special features:	generous bar and wellness area
Rooms:	72 rooms, 4 studios, penthouse
Opening date:	2004
Architecture / Design:	Thomas Willemeit
	Wolfram Putz
	Lars Krückeberg

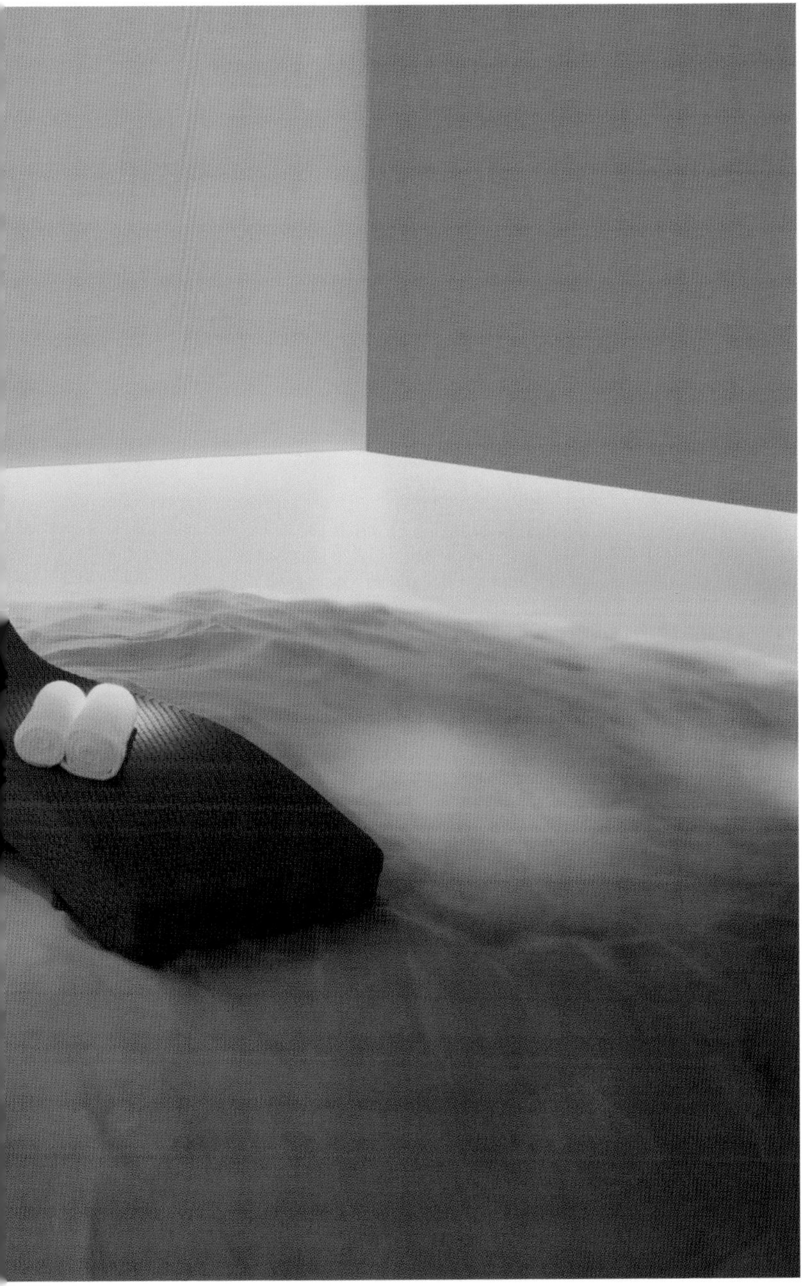

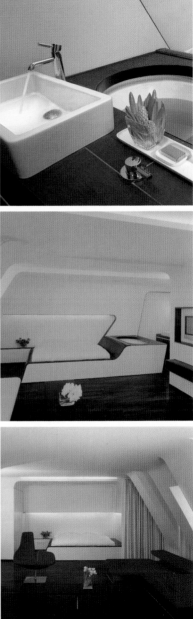

Radisson SAS

Address:	Karl-Liebknecht-Straße 3
	10178 Berlin
Phone:	+49 30 23 82 80
Fax:	+49 30 23 82 810
Website:	www.radissonsas.com
e-mail:	info.berlin@radissonsas.com
Located:	in the very heart of the new Berlin
Style:	urban, contemporary
Special features:	restaurant Heat with show kitchen, Noodle Kitchen, 3 bars and lounges, Splash wellness center, fitness room, swimming pool with Venetian mosaics, bio and Finnish sauna, steam bath, massage and beauty treatments, events for up to 440 people
Rooms:	427 rooms and suites
Opening date:	2004
Architecture / Design:	BHPS Architekten

Steigenberger Metropolitan

Address: Poststraße 6
60329 Frankfurt a. Main
Phone: +49 69 506 07 00
Fax: +49 69 506 07 05 55

Website: www.metropolitan.steigenberger.de
e-mail: metropolitan@steigenberger.de

Located: in the city center, 500 m to the banking district,
1 km to the Fair and Congress Center
Style: functionaly, elegant
Special features: restaurants and bars
Metropolitan Health Club, fitness equipment,
sauna, solarium, whirlpool, fitness bar
5 conference rooms for up to 500 persons
Rooms: 127 rooms, 4 suites

Opening date: 2004

Architecture / Design: Prof. Christoph Näckler

Bristol Hotel

Address:	Ludwigstraße 15
	60327 Frankfurt a. Main
Phone:	+49 69 24 23 90
Fax:	+49 69 25 15 39
Website:	www.bristol-hotel.de
e-mail:	bristol-hotel@t-online.de
Located:	some minutes from railway station, exhibition area and the city center
Style:	quiet, tasteful, personal
Special features:	bar open 24 hours a day
	3 meeting rooms for up to 100 people
Rooms:	145 rooms
Opening date:	renovated 2003
Architecture / Design:	Oana Rosen

NEW YORK VERTICAL

NEW YORK VERTICAL

VERTICAL

25h

Address:	Paul-Dessau-Straße 2
	22761 Hamburg
Phone:	+49 40 85 50 70
Fax:	+49 40 85 50 71 00
Website:	www.25hours-hotel.com
e-mail:	info@25hours-hotel.com
Located:	in the west of Hamburg, 5 km to the city center,
	10 km to airport and 3 km to exhibition area
Style:	dynamic, surprising, seductive
Special features:	bar/lounge, ToGo-Restaurant, Night Bar
	3 meeting rooms for up to 100 people
	lounge, mediation room, sun roof deck
Rooms:	65 rooms
Opening date:	2003
Architecture / Design:	Thomas Lau, Mark Hendrik Blieffert from
	HPV Hamburg
	Evi Märklstetter, Armin Fischer from 3Meta

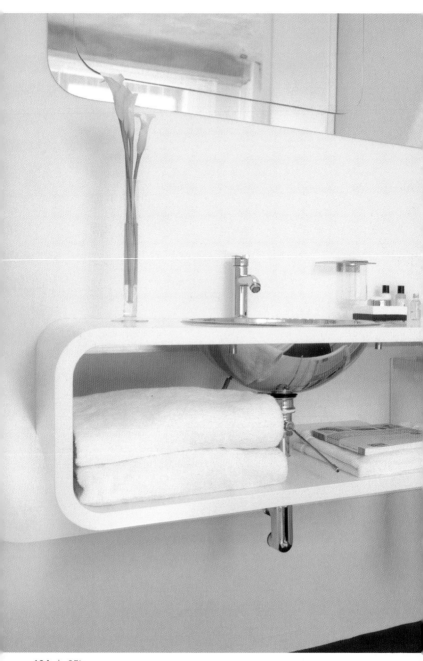

atoll

Address:	Lung Wai 27
	27498 Helgoland
Phone:	+49 4725 80 00
Fax:	+49 4725 80 04 44
Website:	www.atoll.de
e-mail:	info@atoll.de
Located:	directly at the southern pier of Helgoland
Style:	innovative, creative
Special features:	restaurant, bistro, café, bar
	wellness area with swimming pool, sauna, fitness
	2 meeting rooms
Rooms:	43 rooms, 7 suites, 1 apartment
Opening date:	1999
Architecture / Design:	Alison Brooks

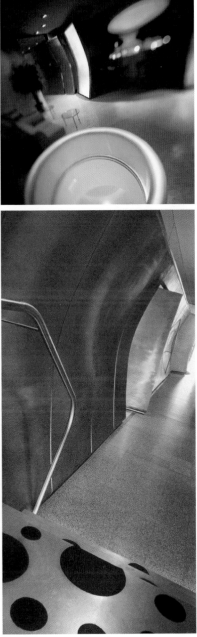

Palace

Address:	Trogerstraße 21
	81675 München
Phone:	+49 89 41 97 10
Fax:	+49 89 41 97 18 19
Website:	www.muenchenpalace.de
e-mail:	palace@kuffler.de
Located:	good connections to public transport and access roads to the new Munich exhibition center and FJS Airport
Style:	personal
Special features:	restaurant and bar, fitness and recreation meeting rooms for up to 36 persons
Rooms:	74 rooms and suites
Opening date:	1986
Architecture / Design:	Peter Lanz

Hôtel La Réserve

Address:	301, route de Lausanne
	1293 Bellevue – Geneva
Phone:	+41 22 959 59 59
Fax:	+41 22 959 59 60
Website:	www.lareserve.ch
e-mail:	info@lareserve.ch
Located:	on the right shore of Lake Léman, 5 km to the center of Geneva and 3 km to the International Airport of Geneva
Style:	tranquil, lifestyle
Special features:	restaurant Le Tse-Fung, bar, spa
Rooms:	100 rooms and suites
Opening date:	2003
Architecture / Design:	Jaques Garcia
	Patrice Reynaud

The Hotel

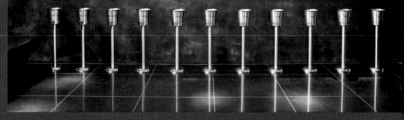

Address:	Sempacherstrasse 14
	6002 Luzern
Phone:	+41 41 226 86 86
Fax:	+41 41 226 86 90
Website:	www.the-hotel.ch
e-mail:	info@the-hotel.ch
Located:	in the heart of Lucerne
Style:	urban, luxury
Special features:	hip bar The Lounge, stylish restaurant Bam Bou
Rooms:	25 rooms including 10 Garden & Park Deluxe suites, 10 Deluxe studios and 5 Corner junior suites
Opening date:	2000
Architecture / Design:	Jean Nouvel
	Thomas Bricci

Greulich

Address:	Herman-Greulich-Strasse 56
	8004 Zurich
Phone:	+41 43 243 42 43
Fax:	+41 43 243 42 00
Website:	www.greulich.ch
e-mail:	mail@greulich.ch
Located:	2 km from the train station city center
Style:	contemporary
Special features:	restaurant, bar, Cigarr Lounge
	conference room for up to 40 people
Rooms:	10 rooms, 8 junior suites
Opening date:	2003
Architecture / Design:	Romero & Schaefle
	Jean Pfaff

Widder

Address:	Rennweg 7
	8001 Zurich
Phone:	+41 1 224 25 26
Fax:	+41 1 224 24 24
Website:	www.widderhotel.ch
e-mail:	home@widderhotel.ch
Located:	in the city center
Style:	contemporary, sensitive
Special features:	4 restaurants, Widder Bar
	7 meeting rooms from 8 to 200 people
Rooms:	42 rooms, 7 suites
Opening date:	1995
Architecture / Design:	Tilla Theus

Madlein

Address:	6561 Ischgl 144
Phone:	+43 5444 52 26
Fax:	+43 5444 52 26 202
Website:	www.ischglmadlein.com
e-mail:	info@ischglmadlein.com
Located:	only meters from the ski-runs and the sivretta ski arena
Style:	tranquil, simple-chic
Special features:	restaurant and bar, fire-room with open fireplace, Zen garden, indoor pool, gym, sauna, Madlein beauty spa with thalgo, thalasso, anti-aging programs
Rooms:	80 rooms
Opening date:	new building opened 2000
Architecture / Design:	Sabine Mescherowsky Gregor Mescherowsky

Hanner

Address:	2534 Mayerling
Phone:	+43 2258 23 78
Fax:	+43 2258 23 78 41
Website:	www.hanner.cc
e-mail:	hanner@hanner.cc
Located:	in the heart of the Vienna Woods
Style:	natural, individual
Special features:	imbedded in a garden landscape, fireplace, sculpture garden, fitness room, library
Rooms:	27 rooms
Opening date:	2002
Architecture / Design:	plan.net Alice Grössinger

Address:	3, avenue des Fleurs
	06000 Nice
Phone:	+33 4 97 07 26 26
Fax:	+33 4 97 07 26 27
Website:	www.hi-hotel.net
e-mail:	hi@hi-hotel.net
Style:	innovative, contemporary
Special features:	lobby, Happy Bar, restaurant Laboratory
	hammam, open-air-terrace on the 8th floor
Rooms:	38 rooms
Opening date:	2003
Architecture / Design:	Matali Crasset

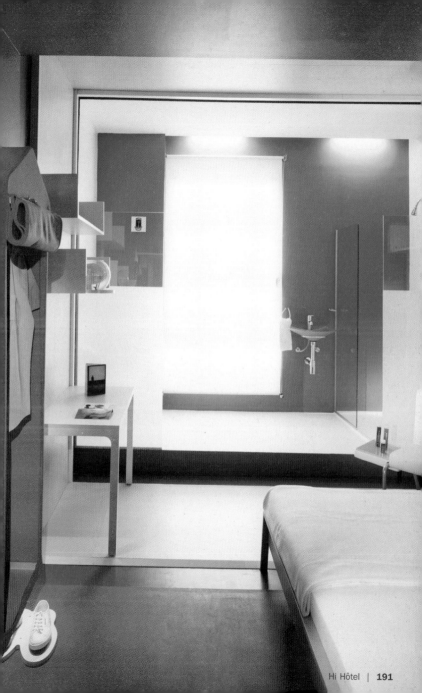

Hotel Casadelmar

Address:	route de Palombaggia BP 93
	20538 Porto-Vecchio Cedex, South Corsica
Phone:	+33 4 95 72 34 34
Fax:	+33 4 95 72 34 35
Website:	www.casadelmar.fr
e-mail:	info@casadelmar.fr
Style:	luxury and elegant leisure
Special features:	restaurant, Carol's lounge bar, snack pool bar
	outdoor pool, private beach, spa and wellness cente
Rooms:	20 rooms
Opening date:	2004
Architecture / Design:	Bodin & Associés
	Carole Marcellesi

Bel Ami

Address:	7-11, rue Saint-Benoît
	75006 Paris
Phone:	+33 1 42 61 53 53
Fax:	+33 1 49 27 09 33
Website:	www.hotel-bel-ami.com
e-mail:	contact@hotel-bel-ami.com
Located:	at Place Saint-Germain-des-Prés
Style:	chic, modern
Special features:	bar, espresso bar
	meeting place for up to 12 people
	lounge with fireplace, library
Rooms:	115 rooms and suites
Opening date:	renovated 2001
Architecture / Design:	Christian Lalande, Nathalie Battesti
	Véronique Terreaux, Michel Jouannet

Park Hyatt Vendome

Address:	5, rue de la Paix
	75002 Paris
Phone:	+33 1 58 71 12 34
Fax:	+33 1 58 71 12 35
Website:	http://paris.vendome.hyatt.com
e-mail:	vendome@paris.hyatt.com
Located:	in the heart of Paris in walking distance to the Place Vendôme and the Place de la Concorde
Style:	luxurious, warm
Special features:	restaurants Le Park, Les Orchidées
	bar La Terrasse, 8 meeting rooms
	spa with gym, three treatment rooms
Rooms:	212 rooms including 70 suites
Opening date:	2002
Architecture / Design:	Ed Tuttle

Pershing Hall

Address:	49, rue Pierre Charron
	75008 Paris
Phone:	+33 1 58 36 58 00
Fax:	+33 1 58 36 58 01
Website:	www.pershinghall.com
e-mail:	info@pershing-hall.com
Located:	a step away from the Champs-Elysées and Av. Montaigne
Style:	original
Special features:	restaurant, lounge bar
	conference facilities for up to 80 people
Rooms:	26 rooms and suites
Opening date:	2001
Architecture / Design:	Andrée Putman

Southern Europe

Italy
Spain
Greece
Turkey

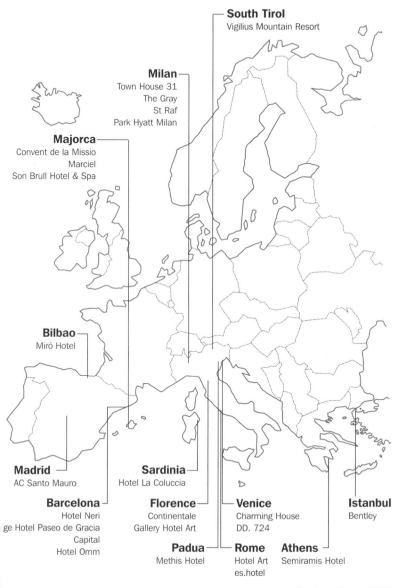

South Tirol
Vigilius Mountain Resort

Milan
Town House 31
The Gray
St Raf
Park Hyatt Milan

Majorca
Convent de la Missio
Marciel
Son Brull Hotel & Spa

Bilbao
Miró Hotel

Madrid
AC Santo Mauro

Sardinia
Hotel La Coluccia

Venice
Charming House
DD. 724

Istanbul
Bentley

Barcelona
Hotel Neri
ge Hotel Paseo de Gracia
Capital
Hotel Omm

Florence
Continentale
Gallery Hotel Art

Padua
Methis Hotel

Rome
Hotel Art
es.hotel

Athens
Semiramis Hotel

Continentale

Address:	Vicolo dell'Oro, 6r
	50123 Florence
Phone:	+39 055 27 26 2
Fax:	+39 055 28 31 39
Website:	www.lungarnohotels.com
e-mail:	continentale@lungarnohotels.com
Located:	immediately next to the Ponte Vecchio, with rooms overlooking the River Arno
Style:	delicate, intriguing
Special features:	bar, roof top solarium terrace, fitness center
Rooms:	43 rooms including one penthouse suite
Opening date:	2003
Architecture / Design:	Michele Bonan

Gallery Hotel Art

Address:	Vicolo dell'Oro 5
	50123 Florence
Phone:	+39 055 272 63
Fax:	+39 055 268 557
Website:	www.lungarnohotels.com
e-mail:	bookings@lungarnohotels.com
Located:	a few steps from the Ponte Veccio
Style:	contemporary
Special features:	Fusion Bar Shozan Gallery with terrace, library
	nearby fitness center
Rooms:	65 guest rooms, 3 penthouse suites, 6 junior suites
Opening date:	1999
Architecture / Design:	Michele Bonan

Town House 31

Address:	Via Carlo Goldoni 31
	20129 Milan
Phone:	+39 02 70 15 61
Fax:	+39 02 71 31 67
Website:	www.townhouse.it
e-mail:	townhouse31@townhouse.it
Located:	10 minute walk away from Milan commercial district
Style:	international, communicative, natural
Special features:	breakfast and outside bar for aperitifs
Rooms:	20 rooms including 3 single rooms and 1 suite
Opening date:	2003
Architecture / Design:	Ettore Mocchetti

Address:	Via San Raffaele 6
	20121 Milan
Phone:	+39 02 72 08 951
Fax:	+39 02 86 65 26
Website:	www.hotelthegray.com
e-mail:	info.thegray@sinahotels.it
Located:	between the Dome and Scala Opera House, opposite to the recently renovated Galleria Vittorio Emanuelle
Style:	personal, illustrious
Special features:	restaurant Le Noir
Rooms:	21 rooms including 2 bi-level rooms, 2 rooms with seperate gym and 3 rooms looking directly into Milan's glass domed Galleria
Opening date:	2003
Architecture / Design:	Guido Ciompi

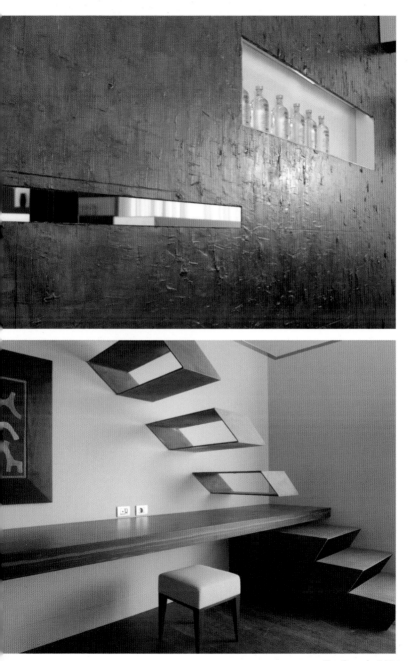

St Raf

Address:	Via San Raffaele 3
	20121 Milan
Phone:	+39 02 80 50 81
Fax:	+39 02 89 09 52 94
Website:	www.straf.it
e-mail:	reservations@straf.it
Located:	in Via San Raffaele close to the Dome, the Scala
	Opera House and Via Montenapoleone
	10 minute drive from the railway station
	20 minute drive from Linate Airport
	45 minute drive from Malpensa Airport
Style:	contemporary
Special features:	lounge bar, fitness, 6 chromo & aromatherapy rooms
Rooms:	66 rooms including 2 suites and 2 junior suites
Opening date:	2003
Architecture / Design:	Vincenzo De Cotiis

Park Hyatt Milan

Address:	Via Tommaso Grossi 1
	20121 Milan
Phone:	+39 02 88 21 12 34
Fax:	+39 02 88 21 12 35
Website:	milan.parkhyatt.com
e-mail:	milano@hyattintl.com
Located:	right in the heart of Milan, just steps away from Piazza del Duomo and Scala Opera House
Style:	elegant, spacious
Special features:	3 restaurants, 335 square meters of function space, designed for small business meetings from 10 to 70 people, spa with a gym, two treatment rooms with private showers, travertine walls
Rooms:	117 rooms, including 26 suites
Opening date:	2003
Architecture / Design:	Ed Tuttle

Methis Hotel

Address:	Riviera Paleocapa 70
	35141 Padua
Phone:	+39 049 872 55 55
Fax:	+39 049 872 51 35
Website:	www.methishotel.com
e-mail:	info@methishotel.com
Located:	in the heart of Padua, just a few steps along a waterway from The Specola
Style:	modernistic
Special features:	open bar, conference room for up to 80 people with full secretarial and office services, gym with private trainer, shiatsu and ayurvedic massage
Rooms:	59 rooms including 10 junior suites and 3 suites with terraces and jacuzzi
Opening date:	2003
Architecture / Design:	Fabiola Zeka Lorenzi

Hotel Art

Address:	Via Margutta 56
	00187 Rome
Phone:	+39 06 32 87 11
Fax:	+39 06 36 00 39 95
Website:	www.slh.com/hotelart
e-mail:	hotelart@slh.com
Located:	two steps away from Piazza di Spagna
	10 minutes walking from Piazza del Popolo,
	Villa Borghese gardens and Trevi Fountain
Style:	distinguished
Special features:	lounges, bar, fitness suite including sauna,
	Turkish bath, technogym machines
Rooms:	48 rooms including 2 suites
Opening date:	2003
Architecture / Design:	Raniero Botti
	Gianfranco Mangiarotti

Address:	Via Turati 171
	00185 Rome
Phone:	+39 06 44 48 41
Fax:	+39 06 44 34 13 96
Website:	www.eshotel.it
e-mail:	info@eshotel.it
Located:	in the Esquiline Hill in the heart of Rome
Style:	young, creative
Special features:	2 restaurants, 2 bars, conference room for up to 510 people, roof-top spa with 4000 square feet outdoor swimming pool
Rooms:	253 rooms including 27 suites
Opening date:	2003
Architecture / Design:	Riccardo Roselli
	Jeremy King

Hotel La Coluccia

Address:	Località Conca Verde
	07028 Santa Teresa Gallura
Phone:	+39 07 89 75 80 04
Fax:	+39 07 89 75 81 28
Website:	www.lacoluccia.it
e-mail:	lacoluccia@mobygest.it
Located:	56 km from Olbia-Costa Smeralda Airport, 50 m from the beach on the north coast of Sardinia
Style:	contemporary
Special features:	bar, restaurant, wide terrace overlooking the sea and the pool, meeting room for up to 100 people, outdoor swimming pool, gym, small beauty center
Rooms:	45 rooms
Opening date:	2003
Architecture / Design:	Julio César Ayllón, Alvin Grassi

Vigilius Mountain Resort

vigilius

Address:	Vigiljoch
	39011 Lana
Phone:	+39 0473 55 66 00
Fax:	+39 0473 55 66 99
Website:	www.vigilius.it
e-mail:	info@vigilius.it
Located:	within driving distance of Milan, Venice, Munich, Zurich, Verona & Innsbruck, 20 minutes from Bolzano
Style:	natural, cool
Special features:	fine dining room and authentic Stube, private collection, wine cellar, conference facilities for 40-80 people, indoor pool, whirlpool, sauna, steam, spa, hay baths, salon, gym, personal trainer, library
Rooms:	35 rooms and 6 suites, all with terraces
Opening date:	2003
Architecture / Design:	Matteo Thun

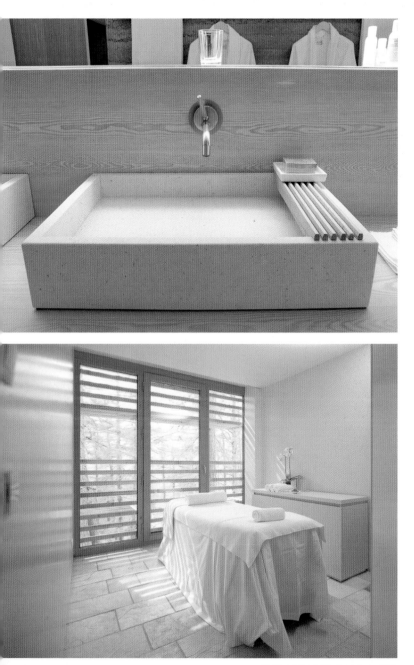

Charming House DD.724

Address:	Dorsoduro 724 30123 Venice
Phone:	+39 041 277 02 62
Fax:	+39 041 296 06 33
Website:	www.dd724.it
e-mail:	info@dd724.it
Located:	next to the Peggy Guggenheim Collection, a few steps from the Cini Palace, the Galleria dell'Accademia and the Chiesa della Salute in the heart of Venician art
Style:	individual, private
Special features:	bar, small meeting room for 12 people, selected library of books of art, countryside and urban view
Rooms:	7 rooms including 3 suites
Opening date:	2003
Architecture / Design:	Mauro Mazzolini

Hotel Neri

Address:	Carrer Sant Sever, 5 08002 Barcelona
Phone:	+34 93 304 06 55
Fax:	+34 93 304 03 37
Website:	www.hotelneri.com
e-mail:	info@hotelneri.com
Located:	in St. Felip Neri Square, one of the most charming squares in the Gothic Quarter, next to the Cathedral and the Sant Jaume Square
Style:	contemporary, exclusive
Special features:	restaurant, private dining rooms, library, meeting room, roof-top terrace
Rooms:	22 rooms including 1 suite and 3 junior suites
Opening date:	2003
Architecture / Design:	Cristina Gabás / Julio Pérez

Elite Plaza Hotel

Address:	Västra Hamngatan 3
	Box 11065
	40422 Gothenburg
Phone:	+46 31 720 40 00
Fax:	+46 31 720 40 10
Website:	www.elite.se
e-mail:	info.gbplaza@elite.se
Located:	in the city center, walking distance to central station, Scandinavium Arena, Opera House and exhibition center
Style:	modern meets classic
Special features:	Svea Hof restaurant & bar, Bishop's Arms pub, The Wine Cellar for up to 40 people, 4 meeting rooms for up to 50 people, business center
Rooms:	143 rooms including the Maharadja and Svea Suites
Opening date:	2000
Architecture / Design:	Lars Helling at Aavik & Helling
	Christer Svensson at Gunnar Svensson AB

Hotel J Nacka Strand

Address:	Augustendalsvägen 52
	13128 Nacka Strand
Phone:	+46 8 601 30 05
Fax:	+46 8 601 30 09
Website:	www.hotelj.com
e-mail:	lena@hotelj.com
Located:	10-15 minutes from Stockholm by car or boat
Style:	contemporary, marine style
Special features:	restaurant J Nacka Strand
	conference rooms
	fitness center, sauna close by the hotel
Rooms:	45 rooms
Opening date:	2000
Architecture / Design:	Millimeter, R.O.O.M.

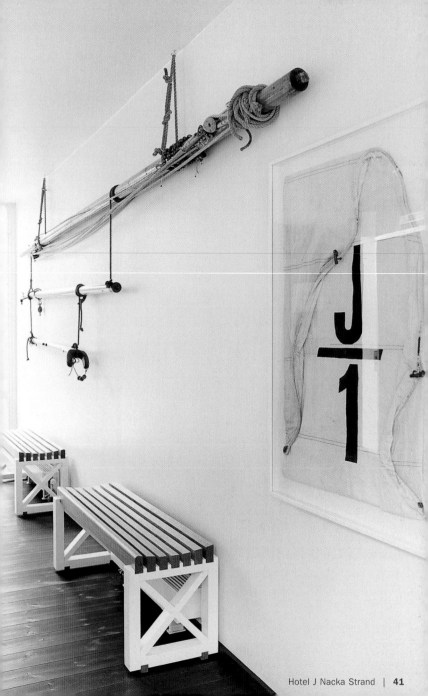

Skt. Petri

Address:	Krystalgade 22
	1172 Copenhagen
Phone:	+45 33 45 91 00
Fax:	+45 33 45 91 10

Website:	www.hotelsktpetri.dk
e-mail:	reservation@hotelsktpetri.com

Located:	in the so called Latin Quarter
Style:	modern, stylish
Special features:	8 conference rooms for 12-250 people
Rooms:	270 rooms including 27 suites

Opening date:	2003

Architecture / Design:	Vilhelm Lauritzen 1928
	Per Arnoldi

Prestige Hotel Paseo de Gracia

Address:	Paseo de Gracia, 62
	08007 Barcelona
Phone:	+34 93 272 41 80
Fax:	+34 93 272 41 81
Website:	www.prestigepaseodegracia.com
e-mail:	paseodegracia@prestigehotels.com
Located:	in the heart of Barcelona
Style:	cosmopolitan, contemporary
Special features:	restaurant, lounge/bar
	meeting rooms, business center
	gym, beauty center
Rooms:	45 rooms including 2 suites
Opening date:	2002
Architecture / Design:	Josep Juanpere, GCA Arquitectos

Capital

Address: Carrer Arquitectura, 1
08908 Hospitalet de Llobregat/Barcelona
Phone: +34 93 445 82 00
Fax: +34 93 445 82 01

Website: www.habitathoteles.com
e-mail: info@hotel-capital.com

Located: just a few minutes away from the city center,
between the airport and the Trade-Fair Center
Style: modern, unique atmosphere
Special features: restaurant, cafeteria, conference and meeting
rooms
Rooms: 103 rooms

Opening date: 2001

Architecture / Design: Julio Pérez Català

Address:	Carrer del Rosellón, 265
	08008 Barcelona
Phone:	+34 93 445 40 00
Fax:	+34 93 445 40 04
Website:	www.hotelomm.es
e-mail:	reservas@hotelomm.es
Located:	in the center of Barcelona's business and
	shopping district
Style:	unique, unconventional
Special features:	restaurant Moo, wine bar and cocktail bar,
	swimming pool bar, Omm Session Night Club
	conference room with a capacity for up to 30 people
	outdoor pool, spa with sauna and steam bath
Rooms:	59 rooms including 1 suite
Opening date:	2003
Architecture / Design:	Juli Capella, Isabel López, Sandra Tarruella

Miró Hotel

Address:	Alameda Mazarredo, 77
	48009 Bilbao
Phone:	+34 94 661 18 80
Fax:	+34 94 425 51 82
Website:	www.hotelmiro.com
e-mail:	info@mirohotelbilbao.com
Located:	between Guggenheim and Fine Arts Museum
Style:	relaxed, personal
Special features:	conference rooms for up to 50 people
	spa with Turkish bath, jacuzzi and massage area
Rooms:	50 rooms including 5 junior suites
Opening date:	2002
Architecture / Design:	Antonio Miró

AC Santo Mauro

Address:	Carrer Zurbano, 36
	28010 Madrid
Phone:	+34 913 19 69 00
Fax:	+34 913 08 54 77
Website:	www.achotelsantomauro.com
e-mail:	info@achotelsantomauro.com
Located:	close to Paseo de la Castellana
Style:	exclusive, central
Special features:	restaurant with private rooms
	8 meeting rooms with various capacities
	reading room, indoor swimming pool, fitness
	center with sauna
Rooms:	51 rooms including junior suites, two-story suites
	and presidential suites
Opening date:	restored 1999
Architecture / Design:	1895 Louis Legrande
	Pascua Ortega

Convent de la Missió

Address:	Carrer de la Missió, 7A
	07003 Palma
Phone:	+34 971 22 73 47
Fax:	+34 971 22 73 48
Website:	www.conventdelamissio.com
Located:	in Palma's old town
Style:	minimalistic, tranquil
Special features:	common areas, lobby, refectory, chapel, bar, restaurant, wine cellar, patio
	solarium, whirlpool, sauna
	meeting rooms for up to 100 people
Opening date:	2003
Architecture / Design:	Antonio Esteva
	Catalina Esteva

Maricel

Address:	Carretera de Andratx, 11 Cas Catalá 07184 Calvià
Phone:	+34 971 71 77 44
Fax:	+34 971 71 77 45
Website:	www.hospes.es
e-mail:	pcalvo@hospes.es
Located:	15 minutes from the airport
Style:	leisurely
Special features:	restaurant, terrace with sea-view conference room for up to 25 people outdoor pool, library, pier
Rooms:	29 rooms including 5 suites
Opening date:	2003
Architecture / Design:	Xavier Claramont